ENGLISH PASTORAL
PARTSONGS

Selected by Paul Spicer

Music Department
OXFORD UNIVERSITY PRESS
Oxford and New York

Oxford University Press, Walton Street, Oxford OX2 6DP
Oxford New York Toronto
Delhi Bombay Calcutta Madras Karachi
Kuala Lumpur Singapore Hong Kong Tokyo
Nairobi Dar es Salaam Cape Town
Melbourne Auckland Madrid
and associated companies in
Berlin Ibadan

Oxford is a trade mark of Oxford University Press

1 3 5 7 9 10 8 6 4 2

ISBN 0–19–343722–8

Music origination by
Barnes Music Engraving Ltd., East Sussex
Printed in Great Britain on acid-free paper by
the Alden Press, Oxford and Northampton

CONTENTS

PREFACE

All my life I have been fascinated by British choral music. I can even pinpoint the moment of revelation: it was Herbert Howells's precious little carol-anthem *Here is the Little Door*, in which I sang the treble part at the age of eight in the choir at New College, Oxford. Quite why this piece struck me so forcibly (as opposed to a more extrovert and exciting work) I am not sure, but the particular quality of integrated vocal sound which his music demands, together with the refined simplicity of the carol and its underlying emotional content, all added up to a musical experience which has stayed with me all my life.

Partsongs are the chamber music of the choral repertory. In this way, they are choral music's most intimate expression: everything is laid bare and exposed. Being unaccompanied, they are also fundamentally concerned with vocal 'orchestration', and the way a piece is 'voiced'—the division of parts within an individual chord, or the interplay of counterpoint— is a mark of a composer's keen ear for colour. This, I feel certain, is partly what spoke to me so strongly in Howells's carol, though I could not rationalize it at that age.

English Pastoral Partsongs is a celebration of the partsongs of those British composers active during the first half of the twentieth century, loosely known as the English pastoralists. All the pieces in it serve to remind us (if a reminder is necessary) of the wealth of colour, variety, and originality that one immediately associates with their music. British composers have often been criticized for being miniaturists, and it is true that many have preferred to work on smaller canvasses—what Christopher Palmer so aptly described as 'the art of carving on a cherry stone'. In my view, however, the scale of a work is irrelevant. Inspiration can be as affecting over twenty bars as over twenty minutes, and that is partly what a collection such as this is all about. It is a celebration of the spirit of the age, and reflects the extraordinary amount of choral activity taking place at that time.

The fact that much of this music has fallen into comfortable obscurity is merely a reflection of a passing taste in our own time. Many of these composers have been roundly derided, particularly by the 'moderns' of the 1960s and 1970s, but in recent years their music has experienced an extraordinary reappraisal and revival of interest, reflected in a wealth of new recordings. That people are now hungry for new discoveries from the period is an exciting state of affairs, and one which will yield much fruit.

This collection is a resource to broaden the repertoire of the enquiring and imaginative choir. With that in mind, three principal concerns governed the selection of pieces: that they should be technically within the grasp of a competent amateur chamber choir; that they were varied in mood and content; and that they should be a mixture of the familiar and unfamiliar. Thus Vaughan Williams's wonderful *Three Shakespeare Songs*, classics of the genre, rub shoulders with long-forgotten partsongs (if they were ever really known) by Armstrong Gibbs, Ernest Walker, Edgar Bainton, Herbert Murrill, and Ernest Farrar. Familiar as the names of Holst, Moeran, Finzi, Ireland, and Howells may be, it is unlikely that most of their music included here will be well known. Indeed, Howells's *The Scribe* is seen here for the first time in print. Early on during the selection process, I decided to exclude arrangements, with the sole exception of Vaughan Williams's arrangement of *Greensleeves* (commonly referred to as a folksong but actually a traditional song), a melody which has come to represent the quintessence of English pastoralism.

British composers of the first half of the twentieth century had a tendency towards inward, reflective music in all genres. It was this, and a predilection for writing lilting music in a 6/8 metre redolent of folk-song, which led Elizabeth Lutyens to coin her memorable epithet 'cowpat' music, an adjective which has stuck like a limpet and which, like all generalizations, is both a truth and a gross distortion. It takes no account of the real range and vitality of creative thought which these composers were demonstrating during this period, or the sometimes rugged and uncompromising music which could surprise and shock.

In fact, I see English pastoralism as represented in this volume as something rather different. It is not just a glorification of nature and a reflection of chocolate-box prettiness, but a sense of that which the psalmist put most potently in the verse which reads 'I will lift up mine eyes to the hills from whence cometh my help'. It is partly a spiritual longing and fulfilment through communion and sympathy with nature. The fact that those 'hills' are the Malverns rather than rugged mountains helps to explain why the music is softer-edged than some of the contemporary music from the continent. There are other qualities too, like a preoccupation with innocence (and therefore loss of innocence), which are all part and parcel of the wider issue of nature as opposed to the corrupting influence of towns, seen at its clearest in the music of Gerald Finzi.

I hope that choir directors will use this music as a springboard for their imaginations. A choir can be as colourful an instrument as a whole orchestra, given the right impetus and direction. To my mind, this should always come in the first place from a real knowledge of the words. Essential though it is to know the notes, if the words are not thoroughly absorbed the piece cannot either be coloured or punctuated effectively. What was the composer's intention in setting the poem? Can we get under the skin of his inspiration? What different kinds of vocal production, vowel colour, pronunciation, placing of parts within a choir, and other considerations, will bring out the full import of the text most effectively? How best can the mood of the piece—both words and music—be communicated to the audience? Can the individual colour of a word add another dimension to a particular moment in the music? It is an exciting challenge.

PAUL SPICER
Lichfield, 1994

Notes on the composers

EDGAR L. BAINTON (*b* London, 1880; *d* Sydney, 1956). He studied at the Royal College of Music under Stanford and Wood, moving to the Conservatory in Newcastle-upon-Tyne in 1901, where he was director between 1912 and 1934. In 1934, he became director of the State Conservatoire in Sydney.

FREDERICK DELIUS (*b* Bradford, 1862; *d* Grez-sur-Loing, France, 1934). His father, a music-loving businessman, was totally opposed to his son pursuing a musical career. Delius therefore began working for his father's firm but, having showed no business acumen, was sent to manage an orange plantation at Solano Grove, Florida, in the hope of redeeming himself. It was here that he began composing seriously, devoting himself entirely to his art. His output is prolific and varied, and the style, which is heavily chromatic, is absolutely consistent and instantly recognizable. Syphilis, contracted in the 1890s in Paris, resulted in paralysis and blindness, and from 1928 he used the services of Eric Fenby as his amanuensis—a remarkable collaboration.

ERNEST FARRAR (*b* Blackheath in 1885; *d* in action in World War I, France, 1918). He studied at the Royal College of Music and for a while was organist of the English Church in Dresden. During his short life he produced a number of works including *The Blessed Damozel* for soprano, chorus, and orchestra, solo songs, and partsongs.

GERALD FINZI (*b* London, 1901; *d* Oxford, 1956). An intensely private man who studied informally with Bairstow at York, R. O. Morris in London, and Ernest Farrar in Harrogate. His overriding preoccupations were with the transience of life and the loss of innocence. This is translated into music in a language which is often sad (though not sentimental) and with a powerful simplicity which is at its most effective in works such as *Dies Natalis* and *Eclogue* for piano and strings. His many songs are regarded as some of the finest in the English language.

CECIL ARMSTRONG GIBBS (*b* Great Baddow, 1889; *d* Chelmsford, 1960). He studied at the Royal College of Music with Wood and Vaughan Williams, and taught there from 1920. He had considerable success as a song writer.

GUSTAV HOLST (*b* Cheltenham, 1874; *d* London, 1934). He studied at the Royal College of Music under Stanford, and it was at this time that he formed his lifelong friendship with Vaughan Williams. Very much an 'original' amongst the English composers, his works show an extraordinary integrity in their approach—demonstrated by the fact that he learned some Sanskrit in order that he could make his own translation of the hymns from the *Rig Veda* which he wanted to set to music. Like Vaughan Williams, he was committed to helping young people, and he taught music all his life, raising standards and morale among everyone with whom he came into contact.

HERBERT HOWELLS (*b* Lydney, Gloucestershire, 1892; *d* London, 1983). He studied with Brewer at Gloucester Cathedral and Stanford at the Royal College of Music, and returned to teach at the College in 1920, where he remained until shortly before his death. In 1936, he succeeded Holst as Director of Music at St Paul's Girls School. Famous early in his career for a remarkable output of chamber music, his life was dramatically affected by the death of his ten-year-old son Michael. After this he turned increasingly to composition of music for the church. His finest choral work *Hymnus Paradisi*, a requiem for his son, has become a classic of the genre. His style has some affinities (stylistically, not philosophically) with Delius, and is essentially contrapuntal, combining spirituality with sensuality in an original way that breathed new life into choral music of the period.

JOHN IRELAND (*b* Bowdon, Cheshire, 1879; *d* Washington, Sussex, 1962). He studied composition at the Royal College of Music with Stanford, and was also a highly accomplished pianist. He became professor of composition at the College in 1923, his pupils including Benjamin Britten. His highly impressionistic style, more influenced by French music than by any English school, is particularly revealed in his piano music. He wrote a number of solo songs, but little in the partsong genre.

ERNEST J. MOERAN (*b* Heston, Middlesex, 1894; *d* Kenmare, Co. Kerry, 1950). He studied at the Royal College of Music with John Ireland. He was a close friend of Peter Warlock and shared many of his enthusiasms, particularly for Elizabethan poetry and folk-song, collecting the latter in Norfolk where he lived for some years. He composed two major sets of partsongs; *Songs of Springtime* and *Phyillida and Corydon.*

HERBERT MURRILL (*b* London, 1909; *d* London, 1952). He studied at the Royal Academy of Music and at Oxford, after which he returned to teach at the Academy. He was director of music at the BBC from 1950 until his death. The sumptuously colourful harmonies he uses in *O mistress mine* reflect his interest in jazz (he wrote a jazz opera called *One man in a cage* in 1930).

RALPH VAUGHAN WILLIAMS (*b* Down Ampney, Gloucestershire, 1872; *d* London, 1958). He studied at Cambridge and the Royal College of Music with Wood, Parry, Alan Gray, and Stanford, and for a brief period with Ravel. Possibly *the* quintessentially English composer, although that description masks much of the truly abstract in his output. His music is completely individual and he was always sensitive to its performers—striving to be 'useful' in writing specifically for amateurs, as well as 'highbrow' in his works for fully professional forces. As demonstrated in the pieces included here, he had an acute ear for the quality of sound and for texture.

ERNEST WALKER (*b* Bombay, 1870; *d* Oxford, 1949). He studied at Oxford and later returned there to become director of music at Balliol College between 1900 and 1925. Amongst his writings is a *History of Music in England* which was revised a number of times, and his compositions include a *Stabat Mater*, chamber music, and songs.

PETER WARLOCK (Philip Heseltine) (*b* London, 1894; *d* London, 1930). He is both one of the most underrated talents of his generation and also one of the most misunderstood of people. Concentration on the more colourful aspects of his life such as heavy drinking and his involvement with the occult has tended to obscure a scholarly mind and an original creativity in his composition. He wrote many wonderful solo songs and a number of absolutely original and quite exceptional partsongs. He was a passionate disciple of Delius and a close friend of Moeran and Constant Lambert. He eventually took his own life.

My spirit sang all day

ROBERT BRIDGES
(1844–1930)

GERALD FINZI
(1901–56)

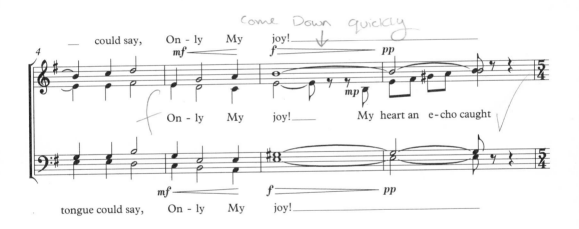

Hide not thy joy. My eyes gan peer a - round,

Hide not thy joy.

Hide not thy joy.

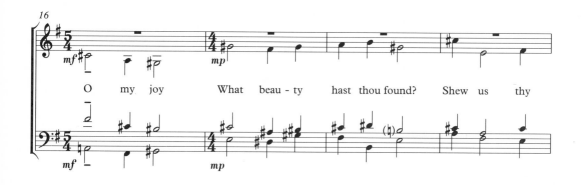

O my joy   What beau - ty hast thou found?   Shew us thy

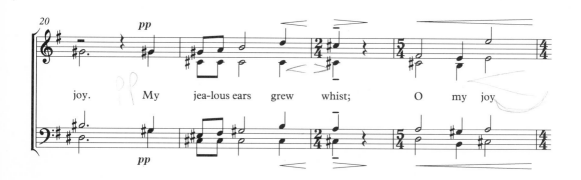

joy.   My jea-lous ears grew whist;   O my joy

Mu - sic from hea - ven is't,   Sent   for our   joy?

Mu - sic   from   hea - ven   is't,   Sent   for our   joy?

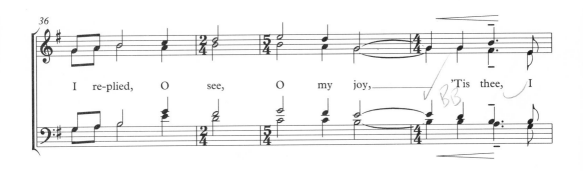

I praise the tender flower

ROBERT BRIDGES
(1844–1930)

GERALD FINZI
(1901–56)

Haste on, my joys!

ROBERT BRIDGES
(1844–1930)

GERALD FINZI
(1901–56)

14

In the wilderness

ROBERT GRAVES
(1895–1985)

EDGAR L. BAINTON
(1880–1956)

The splendour falls on castle walls

TENNYSON
(1809–1892)

FREDERICK DELIUS
(1862–1934)

In this edition some of the composer's doublings between the voice parts have been removed,
to simplify the constant *divisi* they produced.

wild e-choes fly - ing!___ Blow,_ bu - gle, ans - wer e-choes dy - ing, dy - ing,

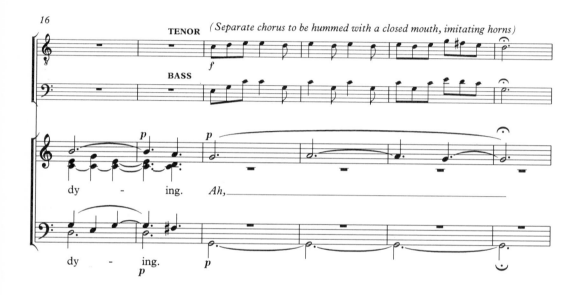

TENOR *(Separate chorus to be hummed with a closed mouth, imitating horns)*

BASS

dy - ing. Ah,_____

dy - ing. *p*

Ah,_____

Blow, bu-gle, blow, send the

To daffodils

ROBERT HERRICK
(1591–1674)

ERNEST FARRAR
(1885–1918)

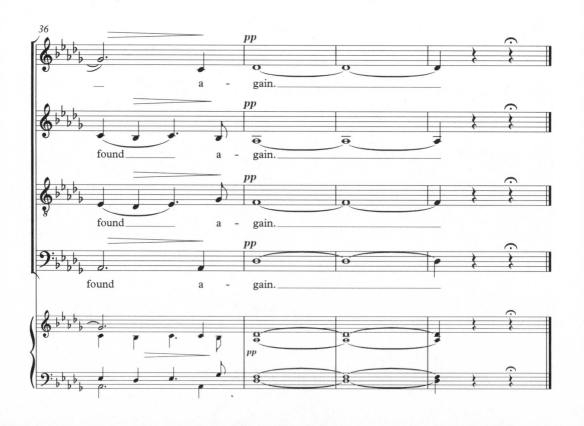

Devotion

Anon.

C. ARMSTRONG GIBBS
(1889–1960)

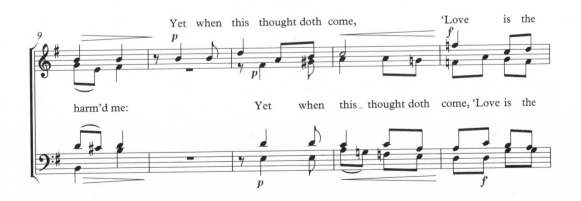

This piece is No. 1 from *Five Elizabethan Lyrics*.

Fair house of joy and bliss, Where tru - est plea - sure is,___

house

I do a - dore___ thee:___ I know thee what thou art,___

I know thee what thou art, I

And fall___ be - fore thee, And

I serve thee with my heart, And fall be - fore___ thee, And

serve___ thee with my heart,

fall,___ and fall___ be - fore thee.

How can the heart forget her?

Anon.

C. ARMSTRONG GIBBS
(1889–1960)

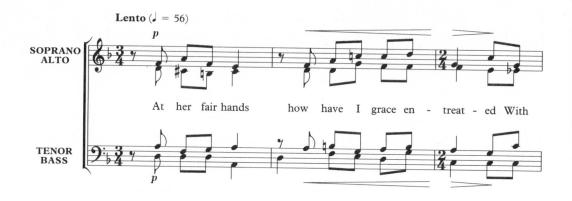

This piece is No. 4 from *Five Elizabethan Lyrics*.

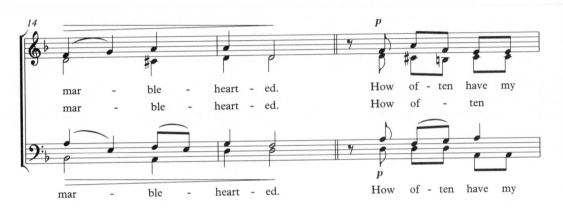

Heart, let her go,____ for I can - not en - dure it—
Heart, let her go, for I can - not en - dure_ it— Say,____

Heart, let her go,____ for I_ can - not en - dure it—

O no, no, no, no, no! She gave the wound, and she a -
____ shall she go?____ She gave the wound, and she____ a -

O no, no, no, no, no! She gave the wound, and she a -

Poco più mosso

- lone____ must_ cure it. But if the love that

hath and still doth burn me No love at length re - turn me,

Out of my

to Conrad Noel

This have I done for my true love

Traditional Cornish carol
from Sandys, *Christmas Carols, Ancient and Modern* (1833)

GUSTAV HOLST
(1874–1934)
Op. 34 No. 1 (H. 128)

man - ger laid and wrapp'd I was, So ve - ry poor_ this was my chance, Be -

- twixt an ox and a sil - ly poor ass, To call my true love to the dance. Sing

Sing

oh my love, oh my love, my love, my love,
oh,_____ sing oh_____ my love, my love,
This have I done for

oh,_____ sing oh my love, my love, my love,

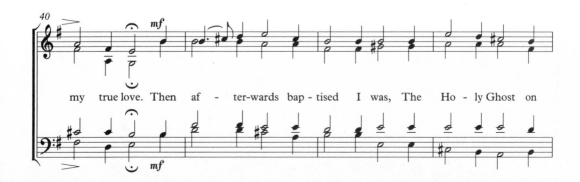

mf

my true love. Then af - ter-wards bap - tised I was, The Ho - ly Ghost on

mf

me___ did glance, My Fa - ther's voice heard from a - bove, To

cresc.

call my true love to my dance. Sing oh my love, oh my love, my love, my love,
Sing oh,___ sing oh___ my love, my love,

cresc.
Sing oh,___ sing oh my love, my love, my love,

This have I done for my true love.___

f *dim.* *p* *mf*

This___ have I done for my__ true love.___ In - to the de - sert

This have I done for my true love.___

f *dim.* *p* *mf*
This___ have I done for my__ true love.___

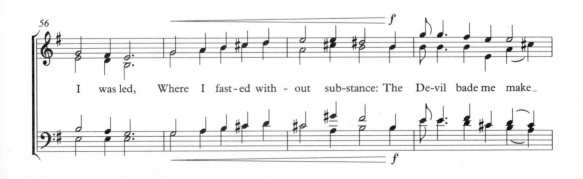

f

I was led, Where I fast-ed with - out sub-stance: The De-vil bade me make_

f

stones my bread, To have me break my true love's dance. Sing oh,_____ sing

Sing oh my love,

oh my love, my love, my love, This have I done_ for my true love._____

The Jews_ on

oh_____ my love, my love, This have I done for my true love._____

Be -

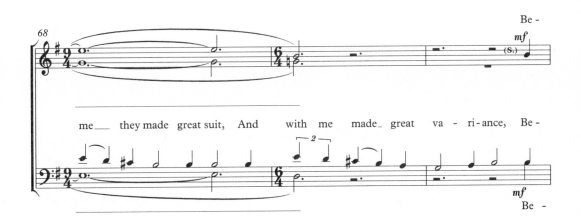

me_ they made great suit, And with me made_ great va - ri - ance, Be -

Be -

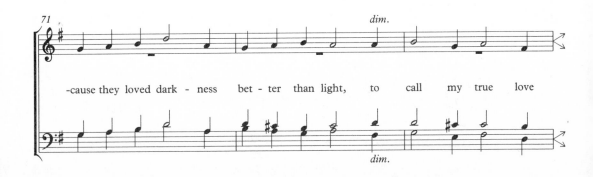

-cause they loved dark - ness bet - ter than light, to call my true love

Be - fore_ Pi-late the Jews me brought, when Ba - rab-bas had de -

lead the dance._____ Sing oh____

love,   my   love,_____ Sing oh____

love,   my   love,_____ Sing oh____

- li - ver-ance;   They scour - ged me   and

___ my love. They scour - ged me   and   set me   at nought, Judged

___ my love.   They scour - ged me   and

___ my love. They scour - ged me   and   set me   at nought, Judged

Animato

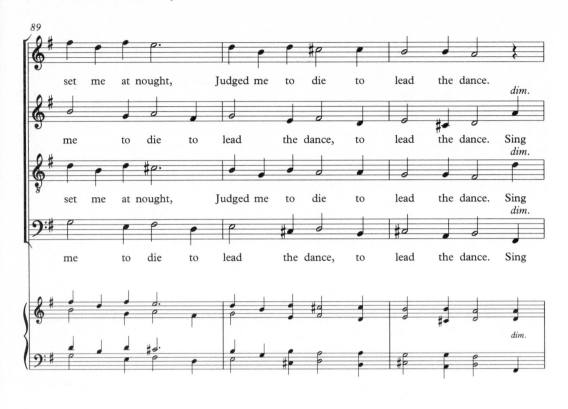

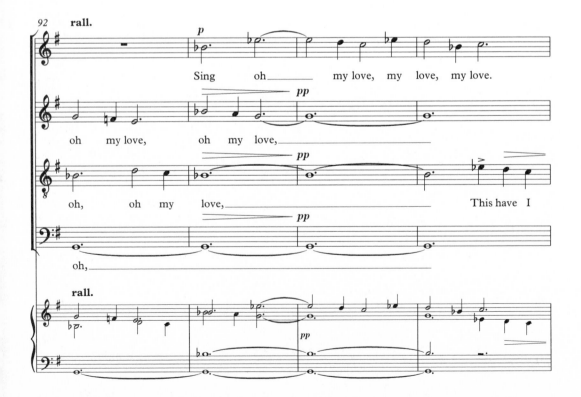

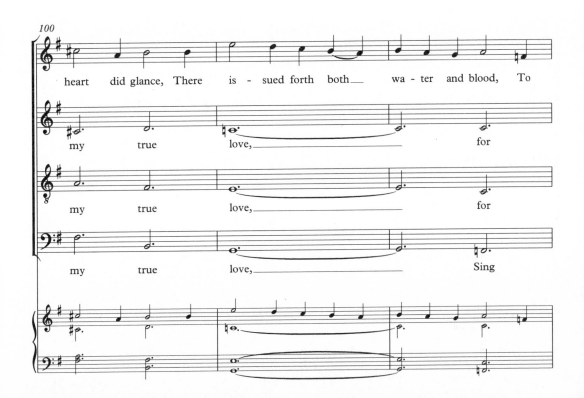

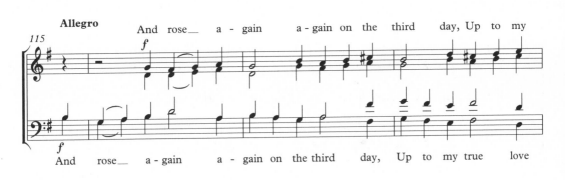

oh my love,
This have I done_ for my true love. Then up_ to Heav'n I
oh my love,
love, my love,

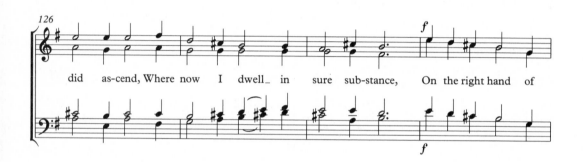

did as-cend, Where now I dwell_ in sure sub-stance, On the right hand of

God that man may come in-to the ge-ne-ral dance.__ Sing oh my love,
Sing oh my

oh my love, my love, my love, This have I done_ for my__ true love.
love, oh my love, my love,

to Mrs Ralph Vaughan Williams

Dream Tryst

FRANCIS THOMPSON
(1859–1907)

GUSTAV HOLST
(1874–1934)

The breaths of kiss - ing night and day Were

min - gled in the east - ern Hea - ven, Throb - bing with un-heard

me - lo-dy, Shook Ly - ra all its star - cloud se - ven.

When dusk shrunk cold, and light trod shy,___ And dawn's grey eyes were

troub - led grey;___ And   souls went pale - ly up the   sky,___   And

mine___   to Lu - ci - dè.   There   was   no change in

her   sweet eyes   Since   last   I   saw those sweet   eyes   shine;___

There was   no change in   her   deep heart   Since   last   that deep heart knocked at

mine.   Her eyes were clear, her   eyes were Hope's,___ Where -

-in did e - ver   come and go;___ The   spar-kle of___ the foun-tain

drops___   From   her sweet soul   be -   low.

The cham-bers in the house   of dreams Are   fed   with so di - vine an

air,_____ That Time's hoar wings grow young there-in, And

they who walk there are most fair. I joyed for me, I

joyed for her,___ Who with the Past meet girt a - bout:___ Where

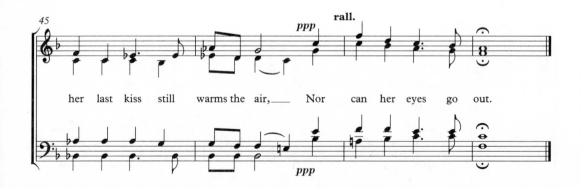

her last kiss still warms the air,___ Nor can her eyes go out.

Composed for the 85th birthday of Ralph Vaughan Williams

The Scribe

WALTER DE LA MARE
(1873–1956)

HERBERT HOWELLS
(1892–1983)

* 'Z' should be pronounced 'Zed'.

The hills

JAMES KIRKUP
(b. 1918)

JOHN IRELAND
(1879–1962)

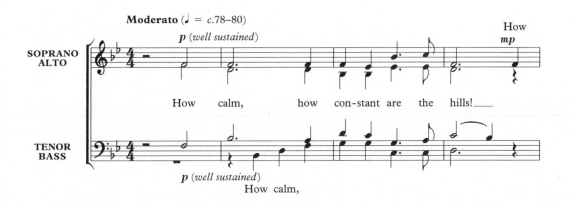

and rain,____ And their pro-found - er ri - vers run_____ From

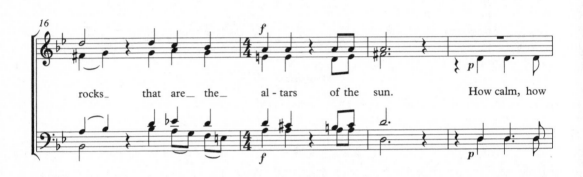

rocks__ that are__ the__ al - tars of the sun. How calm, how

con-stant are__ the hills! Our time's dark gale of ice and fire

Thun - ders a-round them, but re-moves them ne - ver.

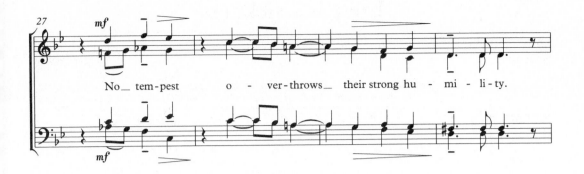

No_ tem-pest   o - ver-throws_ their strong hu - mi - li-ty.

And their stones_____ are ho - ly,
They are both   god_ and tem-ple,   Their stones are ho - ly,

the earth's en - du - ring thrones.   How calm,_ how

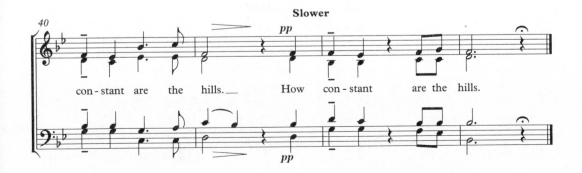

Slower

con - stant are   the   hills._   How   con - stant   are the hills.

Love is a sickness

SAMUEL DANIEL
(1562–1619)

E. J. MOERAN
(1894–1950)

Andante (♩ = 66)

SOPRANO

Love＿＿＿ is a sick - ness full of woes, All＿＿＿

ALTO

Love＿＿＿ is a sick - ness full of woes, All

TENOR

Love＿＿＿ is a sick - ness full of woes, All

BASS

Love＿＿＿ is a sick - ness full of woes, All

PIANO
(*for rehearsal only*)

Andante (♩ = 66)

4

＿ re - me - dies re - fu - sing;＿＿ A

re - me - dies re - fu - sing;＿＿ A plant that

re - me - dies re - fu - sing;＿＿ A plant that with most

re - me - dies re - fu - sing;＿＿

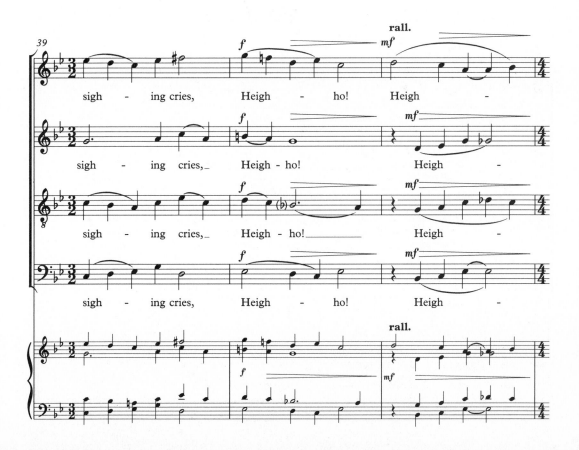

to the memory of Peter Warlock

O mistress mine

SHAKESPEARE
(1564–1616)

HERBERT MURRILL
(1909–52)

to *C. Armstrong Gibbs*

REE SHAKESPEARE SONGS

R. VAUGHAN WILLIAMS
(1872–1958)

1. Full fathom five

The Tempest, I. ii

*Note: 'Ding', 'Dong', and 'Bell' should be sung

Di - ng
Do - ng
Be - ll

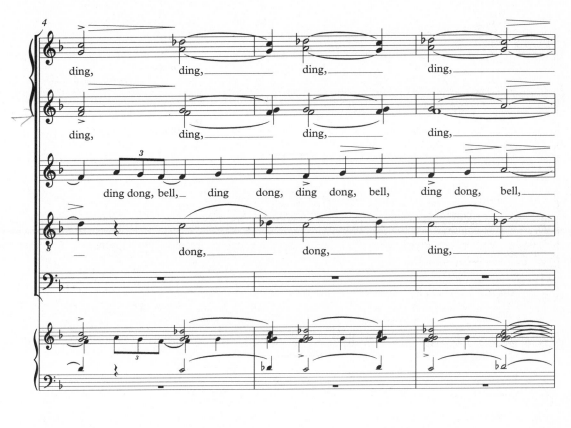

2. The cloud-capp'd towers

The Tempest, IV. i

3. Over hill, over dale

A Midsummer Night's Dream, II. i

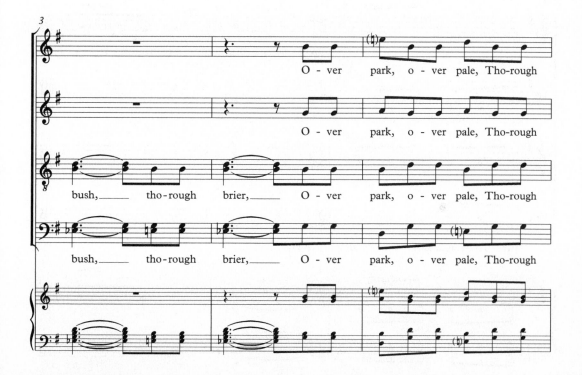

flood, tho-rough fire,   I   do wan - der e - ver-y - where,_____

flood, tho-rough fire,_____   O - ver hill, o - ver

flood, tho-rough fire,_____   O - ver hill, o - ver

flood, tho-rough fire,_____   O - ver hill, o - ver

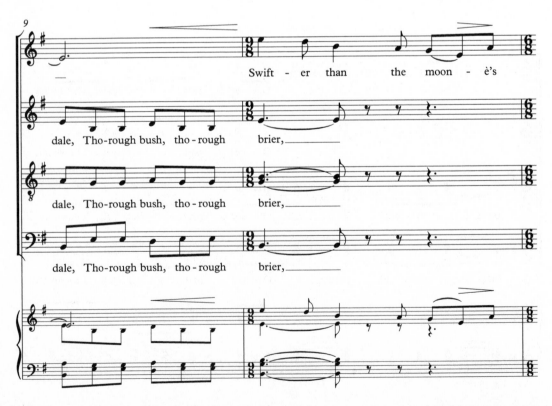

_   Swift - er than   the   moon - è's

dale, Tho-rough bush, tho - rough   brier,_____

dale, Tho-rough bush, tho - rough   brier,_____

dale, Tho-rough bush, tho - rough   brier,_____

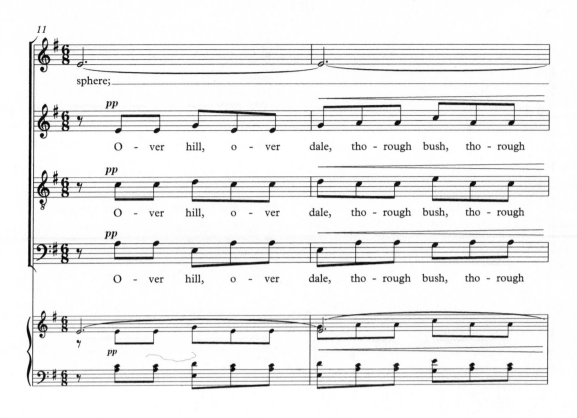

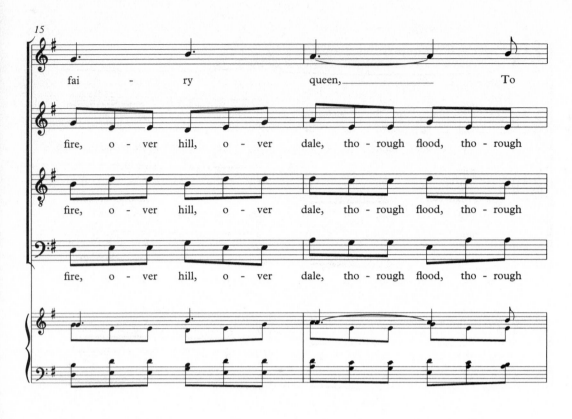

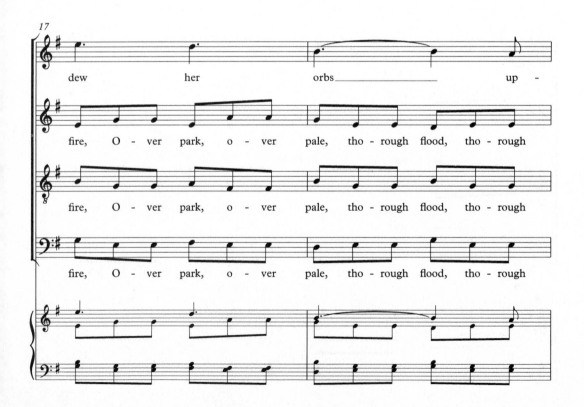

see;   Those be ru - bies, fai - ry fa - vours,

cow - slips tall.   Those be ru - bies, fai - ry fa - vours,

cow - slips tall.   Those be ru - bies, fai - ry fa - vours,

cow - slips tall.   Those be ru - bies, fai - ry fa - vours,

In those freck - les live their sa - vours: I   must go

In those freck - les live their sa - vours:

In those freck - les live their sa - vours:

In those freck - les live their sa - vours:

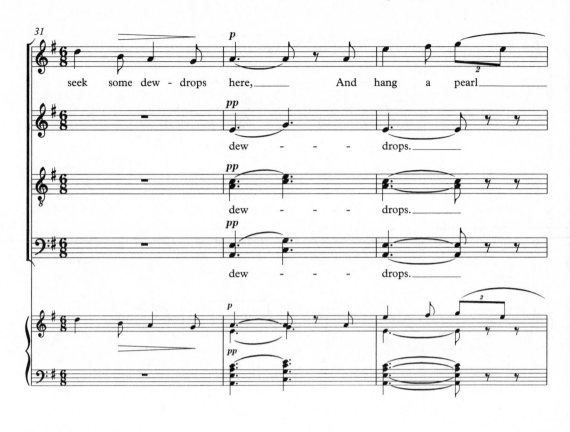

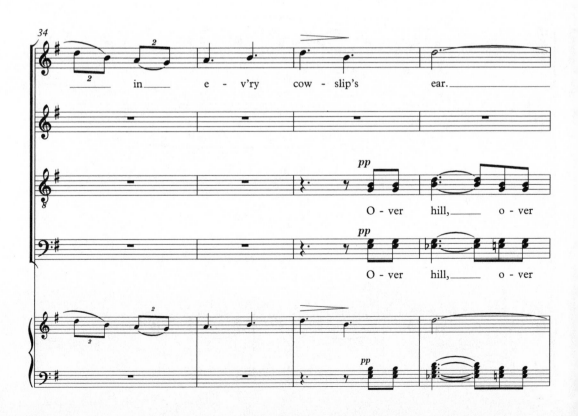

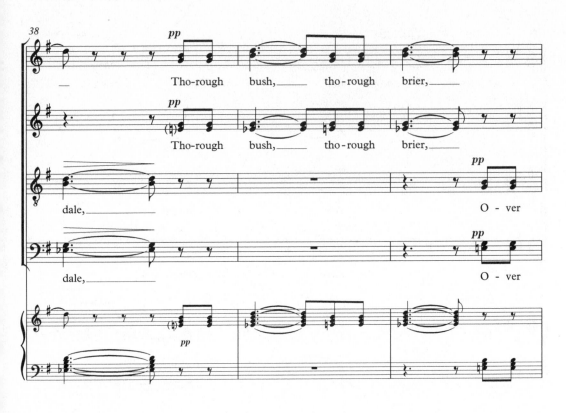

to the memory of
Charles Villiers Stanford, and his Blue Bird

Silence and music

URSULA WOOD

R. VAUGHAN WILLIAMS
(1872–1958)

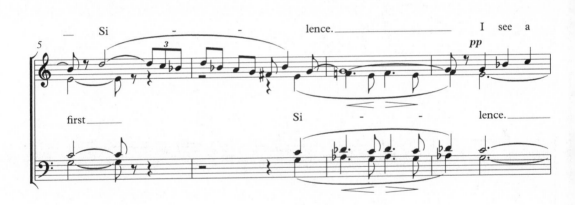

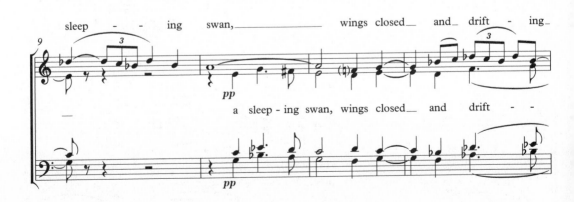

From *A Garland for the Queen*, a cycle of partsongs by ten British composers to mark the occasion of the coronation of Her Majesty Queen Elizabeth II.

where the wa - ter leads, a win-ter moon,_____ a grove where

ing_____ drift - ing,_____ a win-ter moon, a grove_____

sha-dows dream, a hand out-stretched to ga - ther hol - low

pp

_____ where sha - dows dream, hol -

pp

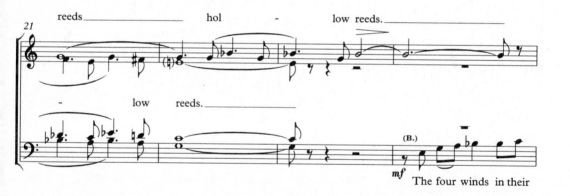

reeds_____ hol - low reeds._____

- low reeds._____

(B.)

mf The four winds in their

p

The four____ winds_____

p

li - ta-nies can tell all of earth's sto-ries as they weep_____

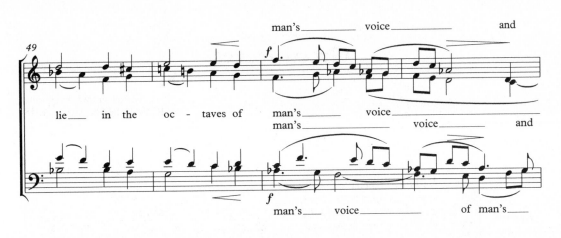

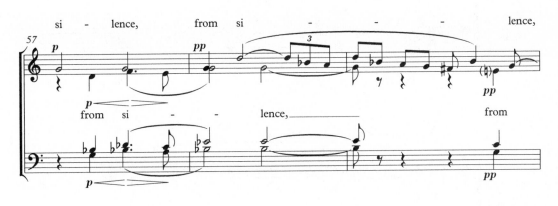

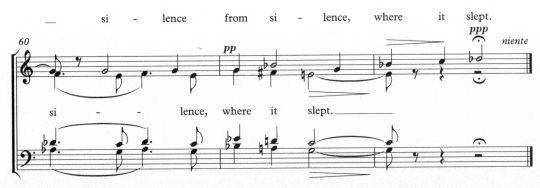

to the Henley Choir

Greensleeves

English traditional song
arr. R. VAUGHAN WILLIAMS
(1872–1958)

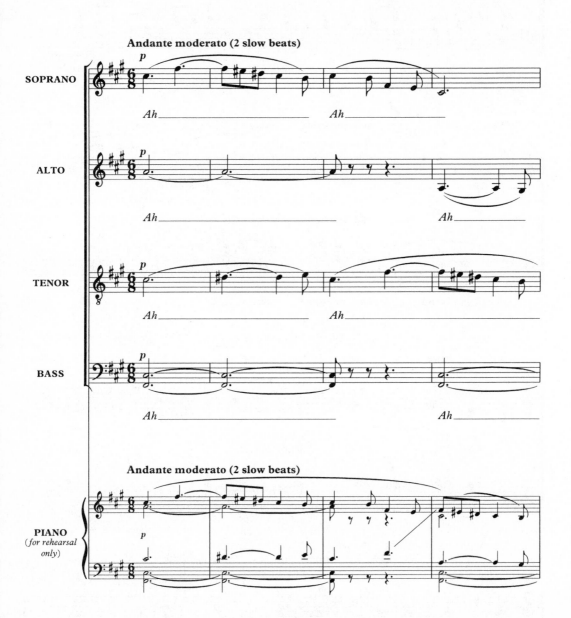

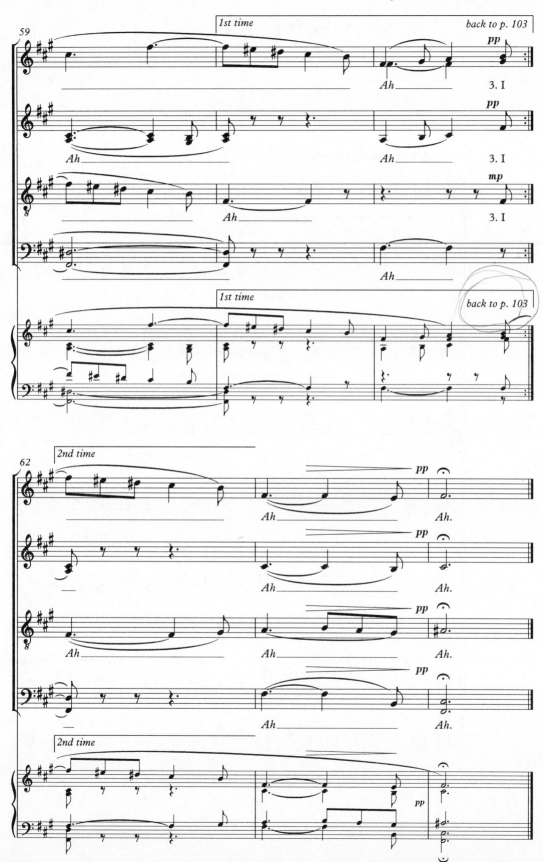

Soft music

ROBERT HERRICK
(1591–1674)

ERNEST WALKER
(1870–1949)

The spring of the year

ALLAN CUNNINGHAM
(1784–1842)

PETER WARLOCK
(1894–1930)